DINOSAURS

PLANT-EATING DINOSAURS

Brenda Ralph Lewis

GARETH**STEVENS**
GS
PUBLISHING
A Member of the WRC Media Family of Companies

Please visit our Web site at: www.garethstevens.com
For a free color catalog describing Gareth Stevens Publishing's
list of high-quality books and multimedia programs,
call 1-800-542-2595 (USA) or 1-800-387-3178 (Canada).
Gareth Stevens Publishing's fax: (414) 332-3567.

Library of Congress Cataloging-in-Publication Data

Lewis, Brenda Ralph.
    Plant-eating dinosaurs / Brenda Ralph Lewis.
        p. cm. — (Nature's monsters. Dinosaurs)
    Includes bibliographical references and index.
    ISBN-10: 0-8368-6844-7 — ISBN-13: 978-0-8368-6844-9 (lib. bdg.)
    1. Dinosaurs—Juvenile literature.   2. Herbivores, Fossil—Juvenile literature.
    I. Title. II. Series.
    QE861.5.L495   2006
    567.9—dc22   2006042360

This North American edition first published in 2007 by
Gareth Stevens Publishing
A Member of the WRC Media Family of Companies
330 West Olive Street, Suite 100
Milwaukee, WI 53212 USA

Original edition and illustrations copyright © 2006 by International Masters Publishers AB.
Produced by Amber Books Ltd., Bradley's Close, 74–77 White Lion Street, London N1 9PF, U.K.

Project editor: Michael Spilling
Design: Graham Curd

Gareth Stevens editorial direction: Valerie J. Weber
Gareth Stevens editor: Leifa Butrick
Gareth Stevens art direction: Tammy West
Gareth Stevens production: Jessica Morris

Printed in the United States of America

1 2 3 4 5 6 7 8 9 10 09 08 07 06

Contents

Continents of the World

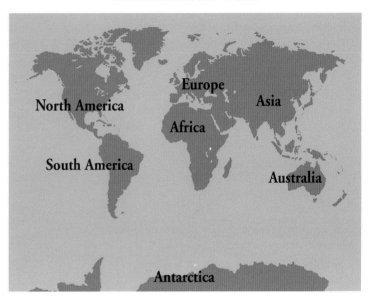

The world is divided into seven continents — North America, South America, Europe, Africa, Asia, Australia, and Antarctica. On the following pages, the area where each dinosaur was discovered is shown in red, while all land is shown in green.

Words that appear in the glossary are printed in **boldface** type the first time they occur in the text.

Apatosaurus

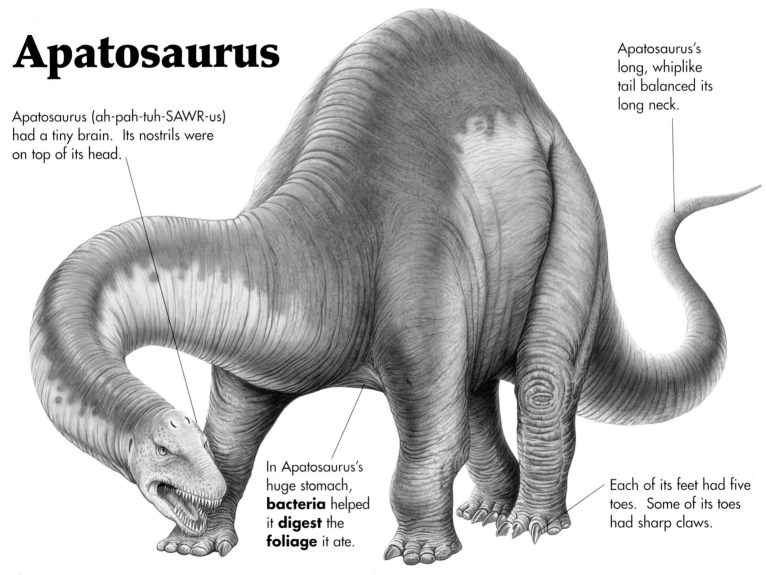

Apatosaurus (ah-pah-tuh-SAWR-us) had a tiny brain. Its nostrils were on top of its head.

Apatosaurus's long, whiplike tail balanced its long neck.

In Apatosaurus's huge stomach, **bacteria** helped it **digest** the **foliage** it ate.

Each of its feet had five toes. Some of its toes had sharp claws.

Apatosaurus was a gigantic **dinosaur**. It could grow to 90 feet (27.5 meters) long, with a huge, heavy body. Apatosaurus needed enormous amounts of food and spent most of its time eating.

1 Apatosaurus was so big that it could easily reach up a tree trunk to get the foliage it ate. It placed its powerful feet on the trunk and stretched its long neck to eat.

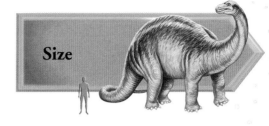

Size

2 Apatosaurus used its peglike teeth to strip the foliage from the stem. Then, it cut the stems into pieces with its other, chisel-like teeth. Because it had a small mouth, it ate only small amounts at a time.

Where in the World

Apatosaurus lived at the end of the **Jurassic** period, from 154 to 144 million years ago. Apatosaurus **fossils** have been found in Colorado, Oklahoma, Utah, and Wyoming in the United States.

Amargasaurus

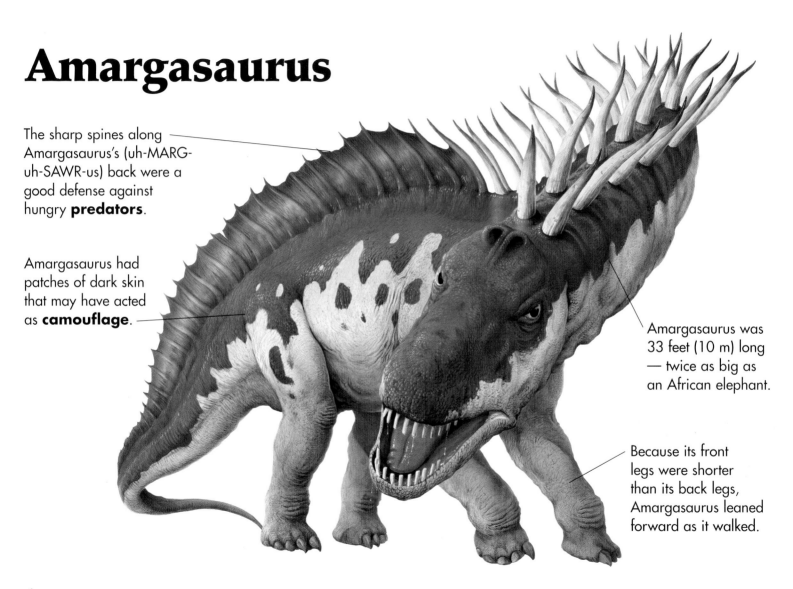

The sharp spines along Amargasaurus's (uh-MARG-uh-SAWR-us) back were a good defense against hungry **predators**.

Amargasaurus had patches of dark skin that may have acted as **camouflage**.

Amargasaurus was 33 feet (10 m) long — twice as big as an African elephant.

Because its front legs were shorter than its back legs, Amargasaurus leaned forward as it walked.

Amargasaurus lived together in herds. Unlike some other dinosaurs, Amargasaurus took care of its young. It tried to protect them from predators but did not always succeed.

Amargasaurus was a **sauropod**. Dinosaurs of this type had large bodies, small heads, long necks, and ate plants. Their feet were like an elephant's, with five toes. One toe had a claw on it for protection against attack.

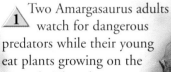

2 The Giganotosaurus wants one of the little dinosaurs for a tasty meal. As it runs toward them, one of the young Amargasaurus shelters under the **belly** of an adult. The other youngster is not fast enough to get away, and the Giganotosaurus seizes it in its mouth.

1 Two Amargasaurus adults watch for dangerous predators while their young eat plants growing on the ground. They do not see the fierce meat-eating Giganotosaurus approaching from behind.

Where in the World

Amargasaurus lived during the early part of the **Cretaceous** period, from 144 to 127 million years ago. No one knew about Amargasaurus until 1991, when the first fossil was found in Argentina.

Brachiosaurus

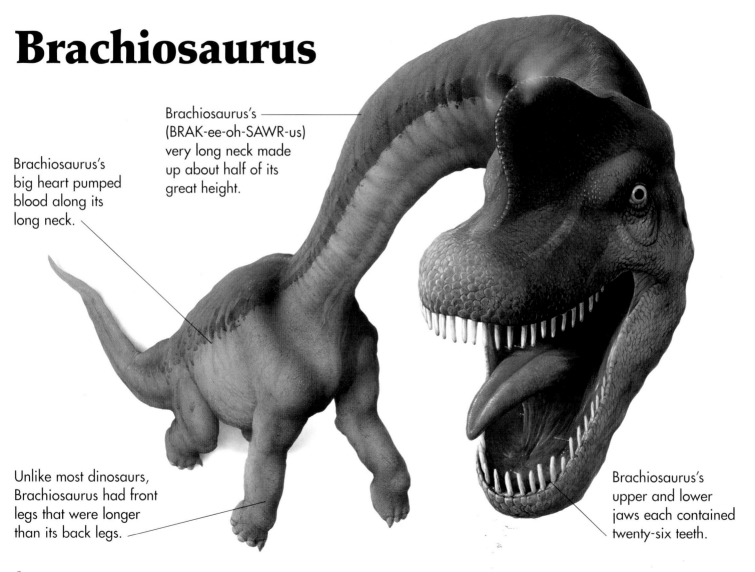

Brachiosaurus's
(BRAK-ee-oh-SAWR-us)
very long neck made
up about half of its
great height.

Brachiosaurus's
big heart pumped
blood along its
long neck.

Unlike most dinosaurs,
Brachiosaurus had front
legs that were longer
than its back legs.

Brachiosaurus's
upper and lower
jaws each contained
twenty-six teeth.

Like Amargasaurus, Brachiosaurus was a sauropod. Brachiosaurus was able to use its long neck in many ways, especially for eating plants in difficult-to-reach places.

Size

1 A Brachiosaurus is feeding on the foliage at the top of a pine tree. Further away, two male Brachiosaurus fight by slapping their necks together. Eventually one will give up, injured, and the winner will be able to lead the herd and **mate** with the females.

2 Foliage did not provide enough food for a huge Brachiosaurus. It also ate plants on the ground, which it could reach by stretching out its long neck.

Where in the World

Brachiosaurus lived from 156 to 145 million years ago, during the Jurassic period. Fossils have been found in Africa and the United States. A **skeleton** was discovered in western Colorado in 1900.

Euoplocephalus

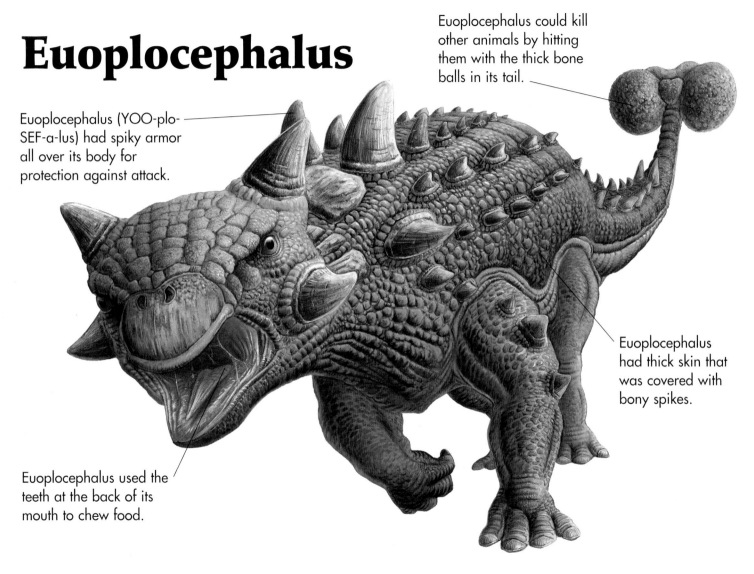

Euoplocephalus could kill other animals by hitting them with the thick bone balls in its tail.

Euoplocephalus (YOO-plo-SEF-a-lus) had spiky armor all over its body for protection against attack.

Euoplocephalus had thick skin that was covered with bony spikes.

Euoplocephalus used the teeth at the back of its mouth to chew food.

Euoplocephalus was not big — only about 19 feet 6 inches (6 m) long. Its thick armor protected it from even bigger and fiercer dinosaurs, however.

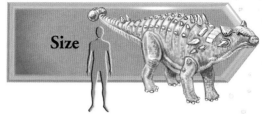

Euoplocephalus had spiky armor plates all over its body, except for its belly. Even its eyes were protected by bony plates and big spines on the sides of its head.

1 While eating the leaves of a forest fern, a Euoplocephalus smells the scent of the terrible Tyrannosaurus rex nearby. At once, Euoplocephalus gets down low on the ground to protect its soft belly.

2 The Euoplocephalus turns its back to its enemy to hit it with the big bone ball at the end of its tail. The Tyrannosaurus rex kicks Euoplocephalus but fails to turn it over on its back. The Tyrannosaurus **lunges** forward. The Euoplocephalus strikes it on the **snout**. The attacker retreats, bleeding heavily.

Where in the World

Euoplocephalus fossils were found in Alberta, Canada, and in Montana in the United States. It lived during the late Cretaceous period, 65 million years ago. It then became **extinct** along with all the other existing dinosaurs.

Iguanodon

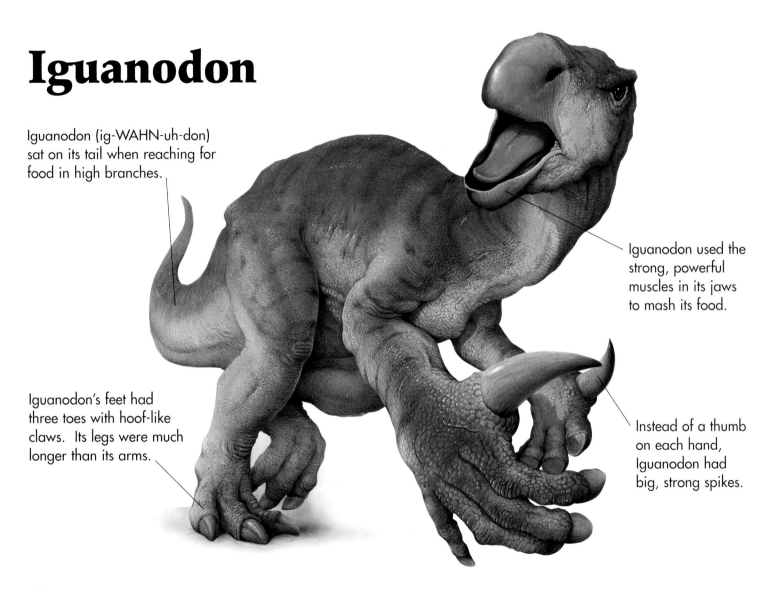

Iguanodon (ig-WAHN-uh-don) sat on its tail when reaching for food in high branches.

Iguanodon used the strong, powerful muscles in its jaws to mash its food.

Iguanodon's feet had three toes with hoof-like claws. Its legs were much longer than its arms.

Instead of a thumb on each hand, Iguanodon had big, strong spikes.

One of the first dinosaurs discovered, Iguanodon lived at the same time as some meat eaters. It weighed 4.5 tons (4 metric tons). It looked like a good meal, but it knew how to defend itself.

Size

1 A Spinosaurus, a meat-eating dinosaur, is hunting soon after dawn. Nearby, it sees an Iguanodon. The Spinosaurus thinks it has just seen a juicy meal.

2 The Iguanodon is surprised as the Spinosaurus attacks and desperately fights back. It hits out wildly with its hands, aiming at its attacker's head. The struggle ends suddenly as the Iguanodon's thumb spike — about 5 inches (12 centimeters) long — sinks into the Spinosaurus's right eye.

Where in the World

Iguanodon bones were first found in southern England. It lived during the Cretaceous period from 144 to 65 million years ago. Fossils were also found in Belgium, Germany, Africa, China, and the United States.

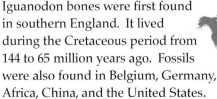

Maiasaura

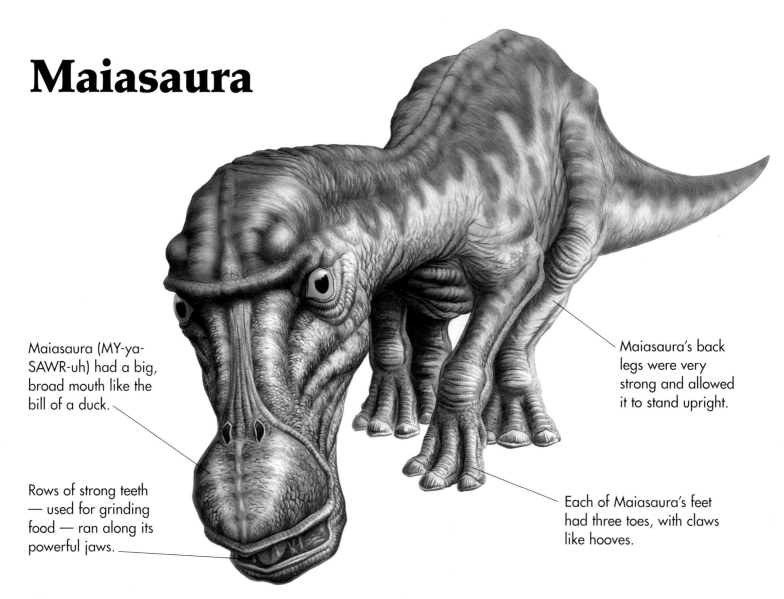

Maiasaura (MY-ya-SAWR-uh) had a big, broad mouth like the bill of a duck.

Rows of strong teeth — used for grinding food — ran along its powerful jaws.

Maiasaura's back legs were very strong and allowed it to stand upright.

Each of Maiasaura's feet had three toes, with claws like hooves.

Maiasaura lived in large herds and looked after their young with great care. Usually, Maiasaura were very successful in keeping their young safe. Most of them survived to grow up.

Size

Did You Know?

Maiasaura was the first dinosaur to go into space. The astronaut Loren Acton took pieces of bone and eggshell on an eight-day mission to *Spacelab II* in 1985.

1 A Troödon, a small, meat-eating dinosaur, watches a large gathering of Maiasaura. It sees many young Maiasaura around nests containing unhatched eggs. The Maiasaura adults normally guard all the nests, but some of them have gone looking for food.

2 The Troödon moves quickly. It dashes for the unattended nest and grabs one of the young Maiasaura in its mouth. The Troödon runs off to eat its **prey** before the parents discover what has happened.

Where in the World

Maiasaura lived in the United States and Canada during the late Cretaceous period, from 89 to 65 million years ago. It was one of the last dinosaurs to develop before they all became extinct.

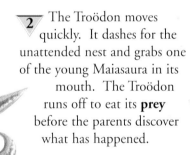

Pachycephalosaurus

Pachycephalosaurus (pak-ih-SEF-uh-lo-SAWR-us) could probably stand upright and run on its powerful back legs.

The male Pachycephalosaurus had a strong, hard skull almost 10 inches (25 cm) thick.

Pachycephalosaurus's nostrils were in its snout, as they are in animals today.

Pachycephalosaurus was a scary sight, with bony spikes all over its face.

Pachycephalosaurus may have looked frightening, but it probably ran away when in danger. If it had to fight, Pachycephalosaurus had a powerful weapon — its hard head.

Pachycephalosaurus may be a **prehistoric** relation of birds. It belonged to the group of dinosaurs called **ornithischia**. Like birds, this dinosaur's feet were pointed.

1 Like many animals today, the male Pachycephalosaurus fought battles with other males. One reason was to attract a female Pachycephalosaurus to mate.

Paleontologists once thought that Pachycephalosaurus banged their **domed** skulls together in a fight. Now we know that their skulls were too weak and would have smashed, killing both dinosaurs. Palaeontologists now believe that each Pachycephalosaurus 2 rammed its head against the body of its **rival** instead.

Where in the World

Pachycephalosaurus lived during the late Cretaceous period, from 89 to 65 million years ago. Fossils have been found in the United States, Canada, Mongolia, Madagascar, and the Isle of Wight in the English Channel.

Parasaurolophus

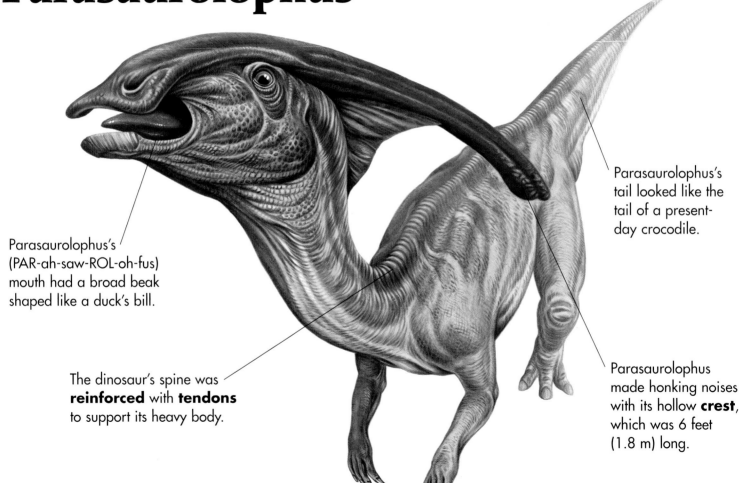

Parasaurolophus's (PAR-ah-saw-ROL-oh-fus) mouth had a broad beak shaped like a duck's bill.

The dinosaur's spine was **reinforced** with **tendons** to support its heavy body.

Parasaurolophus's tail looked like the tail of a present-day crocodile.

Parasaurolophus made honking noises with its hollow **crest**, which was 6 feet (1.8 m) long.

Paleontologists have found only one skull from each of the three different **species** of Parasaurolophus. Each had a different crest on its head.

Size

wing

1 The "trumpeter" Parasaurolophus had the longest crest of all the species. Its crest was supported by a "wing." Tubes inside the crest made the honking sound — which was deeper than the sound made by the other two crests.

2 The curve-crested Parasaurolophus had a much shorter crest without a supporting wing. The crest made a higher sound than the other two.

3 The crest of this Parasaurolophus had a supporting wing, but the crest was not as long as the trumpeter's. Paleotologists first discovered this skull in 1920.

Where in the World

An almost complete Parasaurolophus skeleton was found in Alberta, Canada, in 1920. During the late Cretaceous period (89 to 65 million years ago), Parasaurolophus also lived in New Mexico and Utah.

Saltasaurus

Saltasaurus's (SAHL-tah-SAWR-us) thick armor did not cover its belly, which was **vulnerable**.

Saltasaurus had legs of equal length, resembling columns, like an elephant's legs today.

Saltasaurus's head probably had a rounded front like another plant eater, Diplodocus.

Saltasaurus's tail bones were linked together, making them strong and **flexible**.

The thick armor on Saltasaurus's back was a strong defense against attack. The bony bumps in the armor formed hard ridges. The armor acted like plating on a modern military tank.

Size

1 ▷ A Saltasaurus reaches up to eat the tasty foliage at the top of a tree. A fierce meat eater, a Giganotosaurus, sees it. The Giganotosaurus roars loudly as it moves in for the kill.

The Saltasaurus is frightened by the noise. Its legs fold underneath it, and it collapses to the ground. In this position, it can protect its soft, vulnerable underbelly. The Giganotosaurus jumps onto the Saltasaurus's back. It soon discovers that, even with its sharp teeth, it cannot bite through the Saltasaurus's armor.

2 ▷

Where in the World

Saltasaurus lived during the middle of the Cretaceous period, from 127 to 89 million years ago. Bones from the back, limbs, and jaws of Saltasaurus have been found in Salta province, Argentina, and Uruguay.

Seismosaurus

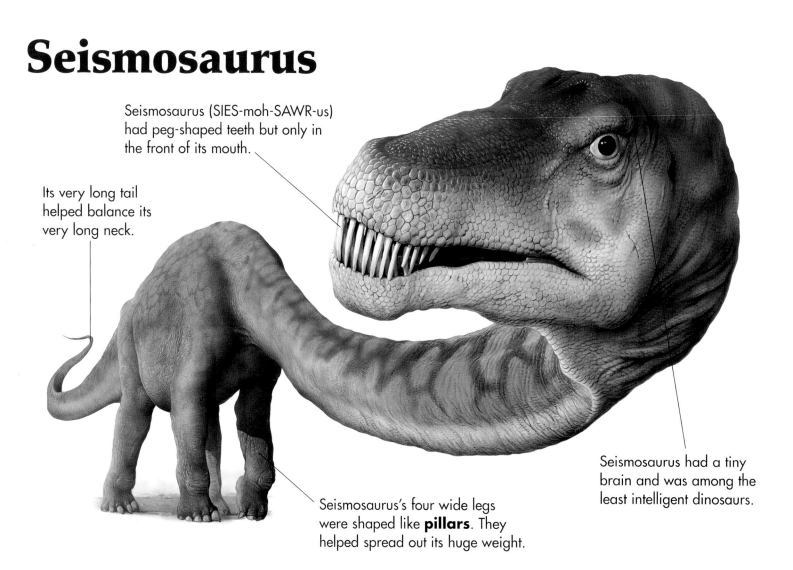

Seismosaurus (SIES-moh-SAWR-us) had peg-shaped teeth but only in the front of its mouth.

Its very long tail helped balance its very long neck.

Seismosaurus's four wide legs were shaped like **pillars**. They helped spread out its huge weight.

Seismosaurus had a tiny brain and was among the least intelligent dinosaurs.

Paleontologists often have to piece together the dinosaur fossils they find. If they are lucky, sand and **minerals** preserve a dinosaur skeleton and keep it complete for millions of years.

Size

1 An almost complete Seismosaurus skeleton was found in 1979 in the deserts of New Mexico. The Seismosaurus had died millions of years ago while crossing a river and was washed onto a sandbank.

2 Dozens of small reptiles ate its body, leaving its skeleton. The skeleton absorbed minerals from the water. The minerals helped preserve the skeleton.

3 Many centuries later, wind and rain blew away the sand, and the Seismosaurus's remains were revealed.

Where in the World

Seismosaurus lived in New Mexico during the late Jurassic period, from 154 to 144 million years ago. Only one Seismosaurus skeleton has ever been found, so scientists do not know whether Seismosaurus lived anywhere else.

23

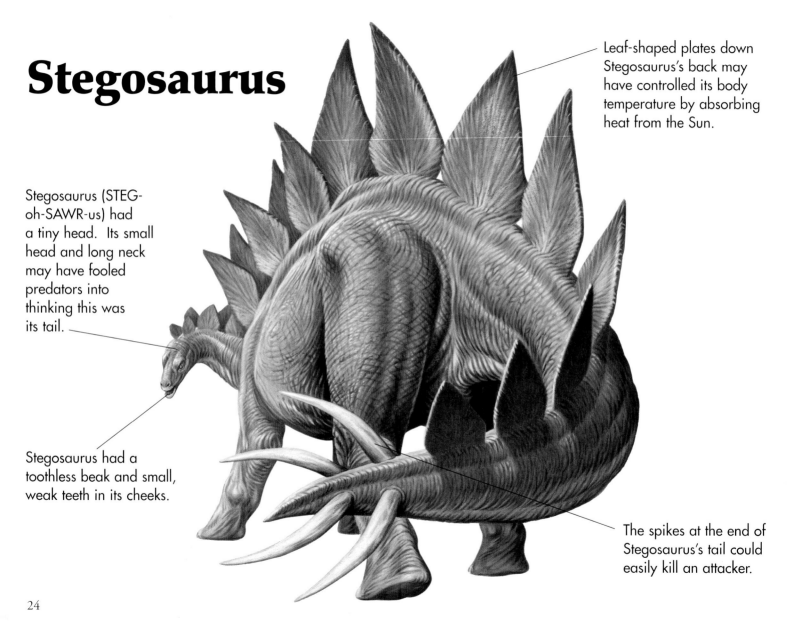

Stegosaurus

Leaf-shaped plates down Stegosaurus's back may have controlled its body temperature by absorbing heat from the Sun.

Stegosaurus (STEG-oh-SAWR-us) had a tiny head. Its small head and long neck may have fooled predators into thinking this was its tail.

Stegosaurus had a toothless beak and small, weak teeth in its cheeks.

The spikes at the end of Stegosaurus's tail could easily kill an attacker.

Stegosaurus was the largest of all the **stegosaur** dinosaur group. It was not built for speed but used its large legs to support its body weight of 6,800 pounds (3,100 kilograms).

Stegosaurus had a tiny brain. Its brain was the size of a walnut and weighed only about 3 ounces (85 grams) — less than 1 percent of its body weight.

The enormous stegasaur was slow compared to other, faster dinosaurs, such as the Allosaurus. An Allosaurus, a fierce meat eater, surprises a Stegosaurus just after it has finished eating a mass of foliage.

|1|

|2| The Stegosaurus cannot not run away fast enough to escape its attacker, so it fights back. It plunges one of its tail spikes into the Allosaurus's leg. The Allosaurus roars in pain. It is lucky that the spike did not **penetrate** its soft belly — which would almost certainly have killed it.

Where in the World

Stegosaurus lived during the late Jurassic period, from 154 to 144 million years ago. It has been found all over the world, in North America, India, China, southern Africa, and western Europe.

Styracosaurus

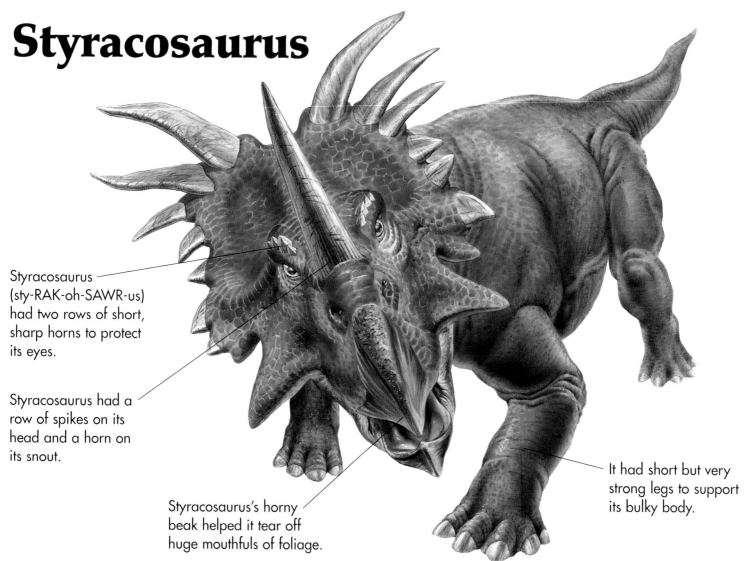

Styracosaurus (sty-RAK-oh-SAWR-us) had two rows of short, sharp horns to protect its eyes.

Styracosaurus had a row of spikes on its head and a horn on its snout.

Styracosaurus's horny beak helped it tear off huge mouthfuls of foliage.

It had short but very strong legs to support its bulky body.

Styracosaurus was one of the shorter dinosaurs — only as tall as an adult human. Larger dinosaurs, such as Tyrannosaurus rex, did not find Styracosaurus easy prey, however, because it had weapons to protect itself.

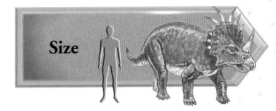

Size

1 A Tyrannosaurus rex sees a Styracosaurus among the palmlike trees at the edge of a forest. The Styracosaurus looks like a good meal to the scary meat eater.

2 The Tyrannosaurus moves to attack but holds back when it sees the Styracosaurus's head spikes. The Tyrannosaurus tries to bite and kill its prey quickly. The Styracosaurus, however, keeps out of reach. At last, the Tyrannosaurus lunges at its prey. As it does so, the Styracosaurus stabs its nose horn deep into the Tyrannosaurus's belly.

Where in the World

The first Styracosaurus fossil was found near Alberta, Canada, in 1913. About one hundred more were discovered in Arizona. Styracosaurus lived during the late Cretaceous period, from 89 to 65 million years ago.

Triceratops

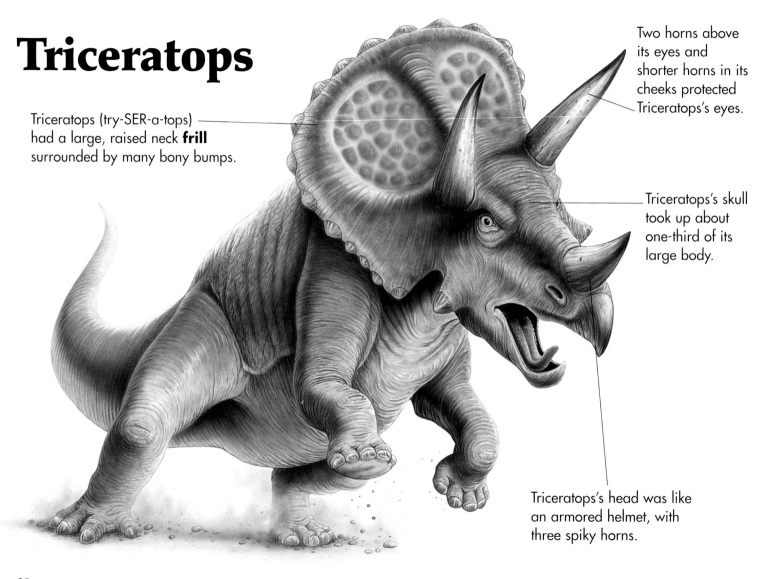

Triceratops (try-SER-a-tops) had a large, raised neck **frill** surrounded by many bony bumps.

Two horns above its eyes and shorter horns in its cheeks protected Triceratops's eyes.

Triceratops's skull took up about one-third of its large body.

Triceratops's head was like an armored helmet, with three spiky horns.

Triceratops was a **ceratopsian**. This type of dinosaur moved around in a herd, had a beak-like head, and a face with horns. Some of Triceratops's relatives, such as Centrosaurus, Pachyrhinosaurus, and Styracosaurus, looked very strange.

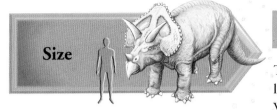

Size

1 Centrosaurus's skull was shaped like a deep box. A tall horn rose up between its eyes. Behind it, Centrosaurus's neck frill had two short spikes at the back and two big holes.

2 Behind its nose, Pachyrhinosaurus had a round patch of bone that looked like a bottle top. Pieces of horn protected its eyes.

3 Styracosaurus had a tall nose horn as well as six long horns and several small horns around the edge of its neck frill.

Where in the World

Triceratops lived in western North America during the late Cretaceous period, from 89 to 65 million years ago. Fossils have been found in Saskatchewan and Alberta in Canada and in Wyoming and Montana.

Glossary

bacteria — tiny living things that can break down food and sometimes cause infections and diseases

belly — stomach, or in a four-legged animal, its underside or the side closest to the ground

camouflage — the pattern on an animal's skin that helps it hide

ceratopsian — referring to dinosaurs that had a face with a horn, such as the triceratops and styracosaurus

crest — a raised line or skin on an animal

Cretaceous — a period of time from 144 to 65 million years ago, when dinosaurs roamed Earth

dinosaur — various reptiles that lived on Earth from 245 to 65 million years ago but have since died out

digest — to break down food in the stomach so it can be used by the body for energy and strength

domed — a raised, semi-rounded shape, like the top part of a globe or a ball

extinct — no longer in existence

flexible — able to bend easily without breaking

foliage — the leaves that grow on the branches of trees

fossils — remains or imprints of animals and dinosaurs from an earlier time, often prehistoric; fossils are found beneath the Earth's surface, pressed into rocks

frill — a border of skin, feathers, or hair around the neck of an animal

iguana — a large lizard with spikes along its back

Jurassic — a period of time from 208 to 144 million years ago, when birds first appeared

lunges — suddenly pushes forwards

mate — when a male and female come together to produce babies

minerals — solid chemical substances, such as salt, coal, and gold

ornithischia — a type of dinosaur with birdlike hips

paleontologists — scientists who study plant and animal life from prehistoric times (before human life began on Earth)

penetrate — to force a way into or through

pillars — upright columns used as supports for something

predators — animals that hunt other animals for food

prehistoric — the time before human history began

prey — an animal hunted for food

rival — people or animals who compete for the same thing

reinforced — made stronger

sauropod — type of plant-eating dinosaur with a long neck, small head, and four legs

skeleton — the frame made of bone inside the bodies of humans and animals that protects the soft inner parts and to which the muscles attach

snout — the nose and jaws of an animal

species — a group of living things of the same family

stegosaur — a type of dinosaur with a row of upright bony plates along the back, long back legs, and a small head

tendons — tough tissue that connects muscle and bone

vulnerable — open to attack, able to be wounded or hurt

For More Information

Books

Dinosaurs. Paul Barrett (Simon & Schuster)

Dinosaurs!: The Biggest, Baddest, Strangest, Fastest. Howard Zimmerman (Atheneum)

Gigantic Long-Necked Plant-Eating Dinosaurs: The Prosauropods and Sauropods. Dinosaur Library (series). Thom Holmes (Enslow Publishers)

Giant Plant-Eating Dinosaurs. Meet the Dinosaurs (series). Don Lessem (First Avenue Editions)

Herbivores. Dinosaurs (series). Dougal Dixon (Gareth Stevens)

National Geographic Dinosaurs. For the Junior Rockhound (series). Paul Barrett (National Geographic Children's Books)

Web Sites

Dinosaur Illustrations
www.search4dinosaurs.com

Dinosaurs Online
www.kidsturncentral.com/links/dinolinks.htm

Dinosaur Timeline
www.kidport.com/RefLib/Science/Dinosaurs/ DinoTimeline.htm

Dinosaur Time Machine
www.mantyweb.com/dinosaur

Kokoro Dinosaurs
www.kokorodinosaurs.com/index.html

Royal BC Museum
www.royalbcmuseum.bc.ca/programs/dinos/index.html

Publisher's note to educators and parents: Our editors have carefully reviewed these Web sites to ensure that they are suitable for children. Many Web sites change frequently, however, and we cannot guarantee that a site's future contents will continue to meet our high standards of quality and educational value. Be advised that children should be closely supervised whenever they access the Internet.

Index